A Boy in 'Akká

(1868-1870)

by
Jacqueline Mehrabi

Illustrations by Malcolm Lee

Bahá'í Publishing Trust
New Delhi, India

Copyright © Jacqueline Mehrabi

First Edition : May 2010
Reprint : December 2010

ISBN: 81-7896-067-8

Published by:

Bahá'í Publishing Trust
F-3/6, Okhla Industrial Area, Phase-I
New Delhi-110020, India

Printed at : J.K. Offset Graphics Pvt. Ltd., New Delhi-110020

Contents

Preface

PART ONE

1.	A Boat Full of Prisoners	3
2.	The Smell of Roses	5
3.	Life Imprisonment	8
4.	Lights in the Sky	11
5.	A Door of Hope	14
6.	Fishing	17
7.	The Puzzle of the Plaque	21
8.	Ninety-Nine Names	25
9.	The Mysterious Letter in the Middle	30
10.	Trouble at School	34
11.	A Good Question	37
12.	The Pilgrim on the Wall	40
13.	The Dervish at the Door	45
14.	A Mysterious Answer	48
15.	Collecting Clues	52
16.	Delivering Bread	56
17.	The Free Bird	64
18.	A Hand at the Window	67
19.	Spies and Another Clue	70
20.	Hani in Jail	74
21.	The Master in the Market	80

A Boy in 'Akká - 1868 to 1870

22.	Telling Salma	82
23.	Remembering	85
24.	A Change of Heart	88
25.	The Sacrifice	93
26.	The Missing Clue	95

PART TWO

27.	The Ever-Growing Tree	102
28.	Mirrors of God	104
29.	The Herald	107
30.	Bahá'u'lláh in the Síyyáh-Chál	110
31.	A Light in the Darkness	113
32.	Banished to Baghdad	116
33.	Everything Made New	118
34.	Knowing With Your Heart	121
35.	The Wonderful Pilgrim	124
36.	A Vision Come True	127
37.	Under the Stars	129

Selected Words of Bahá'u'lláh	132
Meeting Bahá'u'lláh	133
A Short History of Bahá'u'lláh	134
Some Teachings of Bahá'u'lláh	135
Bibliography	136
References and Notes	138

Preface

Thousands of years ago the Old Testament prophets called 'Akká a Door of Hope, but in 1868, at the time of this story, 'Akká had suffered from so many famines, plagues and wars that people rarely thought about this prophecy any more. It was now a prison-city where the worse criminals were sent from all over the Ottoman Empire.

The authorities were frightened of new ideas, and sometimes people who had not done anything wrong at all were put into prison along with murderers and thieves. This story is about a boy called Hani who discovers something wonderful about one of these innocent prisoners.

The Prisoner, His Family, the pilgrims, and a shaykh who visits the prison are all real people. The boy is imaginary, but what he discovers is true. In fact, he finds the answer to the greatest and most glorious secret of all time, right here, in 'Akká!

PART ONE

1

A Boat Full of Prisoners
(31 August 1868)

Hani was sitting with the seagulls on the high, honey-coloured wall that surrounded the old town of 'Akká. His legs dangled precariously over the edge as he spread his toes to feel the misty coolness rising from the sea below.

Far below, baby waves lingered against the wall, reluctant to leave, as though they too were waiting. The boy and his friends sometimes jumped for a dare into the deep, dark water. Older boys would clap and urge them on, while old men scowled and shouted warnings. But today Hani was not looking down; his eyes were fixed on a silent shadow moving on the sea.

He lifted his hand to shade his eyes from the blinding sun and saw a boat full of prisoners sailing slowly towards him.

Others saw it too, and in an instant dozens of

A Boy in 'Akká - 1868 to 1870

children and men were clambering up the wall behind him, scattering seagulls as they waved angry arms and yelled abuse at the prisoners. They elbowed one another to get a better view, and Hani would have fallen unnoticed into the sea if he had not grabbed the leg of one of the men who had pushed him.

"We don't want any more thieves and murderers in 'Akká!" the man was shouting, clenching his fists. "And you, Hani!" he said, turning impatiently to the boy. "Get down! It's too dangerous for you up here! And watch out that one of those murderers doesn't get you!" he added with a grim laugh as ten-year-old Hani disappeared down the back of the wall, his toes searching for footholds as he went.

He jumped the last bit and ran along a lane to the Sea Gate in the hope of getting a closer look at the new prisoners as they came ashore.

2

The Smell of Roses

Hani was not afraid of the prisoners. The whole town was a prison-city and he had been born here and never known anything different. There were guards at the main Land Gate to check who was coming and going and to lock it at night, and the Sea Gate was also guarded and only unlocked when a ship was due.

And in the town there was another prison – a fortress, grim and grey, where the worst prisoners were kept. No one ever escaped from there.

Of course, not everyone who lived in the town was a prisoner. There were many tradesmen who lived with their families in the tumble of little houses that lined the dark, narrow lanes. Hani's father was one of them. He was a carpenter and made coffins.

The boat had anchored a short distance from the wall and the prisoners and crew were already wading through the shallow water. Hani was interested to see how calm and dignified the prisoners were: no shouting, and everyone helping one another.

There were several veiled women among them. The sailors suggested that they carry the women on their backs to the shore so they would not get wet. One of the young men among the prisoners objected, saying it was not dignified for them to be carried in this manner. He asked for a wooden chair to be brought so that they could sit on it and be carried more comfortably over the water.

The young man had a handsome and sensitive face which Hani thought was both kind and sad at the same time. He had a feeling that the sadness was because of the suffering of those around him.

The Smell of Roses

There were also a number of children and babies. Hani was puzzled and wondered what their parents could have done that was so bad they had been sent to such a dreadful place as this.

The guards hurried the exhausted prisoners along the dirty street. Hani thought there were about seventy in all. One of the young women swayed as though she was going to faint, and the young man and a youth who looked like him reached out to help her. Hani guessed she was their sister.

A gang of boys laughed and threw rotten fruit at the prisoners. But Hani felt sad. Something was wrong. They did not look like criminals. So why had they been sent as prisoners to 'Akká?

At the head of the group a distinguished Figure was walking with a light step towards the prison-fortress. His long black hair flowed from beneath His turban and His cloak floated behind Him. Although He was simply dressed, Hani thought He was like a King. The other prisoners were following as though all that mattered was to be close to Him.

Something made Hani look around in surprise. Instead of the smell of fish that usually hung over the city, there was a definite smell of roses.

3

Life Imprisonment

"I can't remember when I last smelled a rose!" laughed Hani's mother when he told her what had happened. Not many flowers grew in the town.

"Must be that over-active imagination of yours!" she said, putting a bowl of bean stew on a low, round table, which was surrounded with colourful cushions for everyone to sit on. Although the house was small and in a poor part of town, it was bright and welcoming inside with its white-washed walls and a samovar bubbling away in a corner boiling water for making tea.

Hani's older brother, Fuad, was also laughing, but not unkindly. He knew Hani often felt things he did not.

Hani was thinking. Perhaps the scent of roses had not come from flowers at all but from the spiritual feeling he'd had when he saw the prisoner who looked like a King? It was something holy.

Life Imprisonment

As they began their meal, his father said, "I heard that these new prisoners planned to overthrow the government and are very dangerous and have been sentenced to life-imprisonment."

"They didn't look dangerous," said Hani as he broke off a piece of bread and wrapped it round some beans and popped it in his mouth.

"How could you tell?" asked Salma, his sister, her large black eyes turned expectantly towards him. She was eight years old and being a girl was not allowed to go out on her own, so Hani was her passport to freedom and adventure. In another year she knew she would probably not be allowed out at all unless it was with her mother and only then if she wore a veil. One of her cousins had even been married when she was nine, although Salma knew that would not happen to her because her mother did not agree with the custom of girls marrying so young. Fifteen was early enough, her mother said.

A Boy in 'Akká - 1868 to 1870

"They were kind to each other," said Hani in answer to Salma's question. "And there were children and babies."

But it was not just that, he thought to himself, and decided to talk about it later with his father.

4

Lights in the Sky

The next day, as Hani was sweeping the sawdust in his father's workshop at the back of the house, he said, "I think I saw something the other night."

His father uttered a questioning "Mmm?" while shaving a rough piece of wood off a coffin.

"Lights in the sky," said Hani. "Like banners."

"Oh?" His father rubbed the side of the coffin with his thumb to see if it was smooth enough.

"Above the town," added Hani.

A Boy in 'Akká - 1868 to 1870

Yunus stopped work for a second to look across at his son.

"A dream?" he asked. People in the town took dreams seriously and it was a favourite pastime of the women in particular to try to interpret their meaning. Only the week before, his wife, Pari, had dreamed one of her teeth had fallen out, and she said that meant someone in the family had died. Sure enough, two days later they heard that an aunt had died in Haifa, across the bay from 'Akká.

"Not a dream," said Hani. "I woke up in the middle of the night and the sky was full of light."

This was interesting indeed, thought Yunus. 'Akká was such a dirty little town, full of rubbish and disease. There was a saying that if a bird flew over it, it would drop dead before it got to the other side. The thought of banners of light shining above the town gave him a warm feeling of hope.

"So. These lights," he said. "What do you think they were?"

"I thought they must be a sign," said Hani, uncertainly. "And that they were welcoming something or someone special to our town. That's why I was waiting on the wall. To see what it was."

Lights in the Sky

"And you thought it might have something to do with those prisoners?"

"Yes."

"But someone from God would not be a criminal," observed Yunus, not wanting to disillusion his son but not wanting to encourage him either in case he was wrong.

"I know," said Hani, "but they were different from other prisoners."

He told his father about the regal Figure and the other people he had seen.

"Which means that if the lights were banners welcoming them, then they aren't criminals at all even though people say they are," he said, looking anxiously at his father, hoping with all his heart that he would agree.

"Are you sure you saw the lights?" asked Yunus.

"Well...," Hani hesitated. "I *felt* I did!"

"I'll see what I can find out," Yunus assured him. "But don't say anything to anyone or we could be put in prison too!"

Hani thought he would not mind so long as he was with the young man and the one who seemed to be the Leader.

5

A Door of Hope

Yunus was in one of the small rooms around the courtyard of a mosque where some of the mullás taught their students, and he had just asked one of them about the lights Hani thought he had seen.

"Just the boy's imagination!" exclaimed the mullá, looking up from several sheets of paper spread over the table in front of him. He was busy writing an explanation about angels that were said to come to earth with every drop of rain.

"Idle fancies! Forget it!" added the mullá, annoyed at being interrupted. He told Yunus about the important subject he was writing about.

A Door of Hope

At the mullá's words, Yunus smiled. Angels bringing raindrops to earth? Now that is what he would call an idle fancy! But he waited respectfully for a few minutes before saying anything more. People were expected to accept what the mullás said without question because they were supposed to be the authorities on all things religious. However, there was something about Hani's experience that made Yunus feel it was true and he could not keep quiet forever.

"I was thinking about all the prophecies that say wonderful things about 'Akká," he said cautiously. "And I wonder if they are about to happen?"

The mullá looked up and gazed at Yunus from beneath bushy black eyebrows that collided in the middle of his forehead, giving him a rather fierce look, although really he was a gentle man and just wanted a quiet life. He knew about the prophecies, of course. Everyone did. They said things like "'Akká is a city ... to which God has shown His special mercy", and that whoever enters 'Akká, "longing for it and eager to visit it, God will forgive his sins, both of the past and of the future". It was an amazing promise.

"Even the old prophets spoke about 'Akká three thousand years ago," Yunus reminded the mullá. "About it being a door of hope."

Yunus also knew that the prophets said troubles would be turned into joy, despair into hope, and that there would be singing in the valley of 'Akká. But he had a feeling the mullá was not really interested.

To be truthful, the mullá did not know the answer to Yunus's question about whether the prophecies were about to come true or not. But he did not want to admit it. Nor to admit that anything seen by a ten-year-old boy could be taken seriously. If anyone should be seeing things it was him, not a boy who ran barefoot through the streets of 'Akká and was not even one of his students.

Anyway, 'Akká was such a poor little town he could not imagine why God said it was so special. He decided to read more about the prophecies one day and see what other religious scholars had to say. He would do it after he had finished writing about the angels and raindrops idea.

He began shuffling his papers and Yunus knew it was time to leave. He said nothing about Hani's feeling that the newly-arrived prisoners had something to do with the banners of light, feeling sure the mullá would dismiss that too.

6

Fishing

The city was alive with rumours about the new prisoners.

"People say they look very fierce!" Hani's cousin Baz told him breathlessly, having run from the other side of town with the latest news. He and Hani were the same age and the best of friends.

"No they don't!" said Hani.

"And they tried to fight the guards when they landed!" continued Baz.

"No they didn't!" said Hani.

Baz stopped for a second. "But everyone is saying it," he protested. "Even in the mosques."

"It's not true, though," said Hani.

"How do you know?"

"Because I saw them."

He described how dignified and calm the prisoners had been.

"And there weren't just men," he added, "but women and children too."

"Then why are they being locked up?" asked Baz, still not convinced.

"I don't know," admitted Hani. "But I wish I could rescue them!"

They both knew that was impossible. The fortress where the prisoners were being kept was huge, with few windows and thick stone walls. It was pitted with dents made by cannon balls from attacks launched against it in the past. One of these attacks had come from Napoleon Bonaparte who had tried to invade the city in 1799, nearly seventy years before. Hani had often imagined the sight of the French fleet out at sea, white sails billowing in the wind, and exploding puffs of black smoke as cannon balls flew through the air to bounce off the walls of the fortress. After two months Napoleon had given up and sailed to India instead.

Hani was silent for so long Baz grew restless and began to draw a circle in the dust with his big toe.

"How about going fishing?" he suggested.

Fishing

Hani called his sister and the three of them ran until they came to a wide part of the outer wall that surrounded the town, not far from the fortress.

Climbing down the other side they made their way over slippery black rocks until they came to deeper water. Baz was carrying an old fishing net they had found washed up on the beach a while ago. Hani put a handful of pebbles into the bottom so it would sink just below the surface and tied a piece of stale bread into a corner as bait, then lowered it into the water. They took turns to hold it and waited for a fish to swim in.

A Boy in 'Akká - 1868 to 1870

An hour later they were still waiting and were just about to give up when there was a sudden tug on the net. Salma was holding it at the time and her fingers were so cold she nearly let go. Plunging their arms into the water, the boys managed to pull the net onto the rocks to see what they had caught. It was not a fish as they had expected but a very old tin box, with something that rattled inside.

7

The Puzzle of the Plaque

"What is it?" asked Salma, as the children prised open the tin box with a shell.

Baz emptied the water that had leaked in through the rusty hinges, and a round metal plaque fell out.

"There's something engraved on it," said Hani, picking it up to have a closer look and finding that it fitted neatly into the palm of his hand.

Tiny words covered the plaque, surrounding a small circle in the centre. The engravings were very fine and almost rubbed smooth from being tossed about in the box of salty water.

They gazed at it for a while, unable to decipher what it meant.

Hani lightly touched the circle in the middle and paused as he felt a slight roughness. He looked at it more closely.

"I think there is a letter in the middle," he said. "But it's too faint to make out. We'll try and find out what it means later. Meanwhile, it can be our lucky sign."

The others nodded.

Baz picked up the rusty box. "I'll try to clean this up," he said, "and then we can keep the plaque in here. And other things," he added vaguely, not sure what those might be.

A loud shout made them jump and almost drop both the box and the plaque. One of the soldiers patrolling the walls of the city had noticed them down on the rocks. He waved his rifle, indicating they should come back. The soldiers usually allowed children and the other townsfolk to fish off the rocks outside the wall, but this soldier was new.

Hani put the plaque in his pocket as they hastily picked their way back over the wet rocks.

When they came to the foot of the wall the soldier glowered down at them, and Salma began to cry. Hani held up the net so the soldier could see it.

"We were fishing," he said.

The soldier had been bored walking up and down the city wall and decided he would give the children a scare for going on the beach. He was young, eighteen or so, and felt important dressed in his new uniform and cap and carrying a gun.

"Don't speak!" he shouted, and ordered them to climb over the wall and walk in front of him back into the town. Every now and then he prodded the boys with the point of his rifle.

As they stumbled along, being poked in the back every few steps, the children knew it would be safer to keep quiet and not protest, so they said nothing. Hani did not think the soldier would shoot them, but he did feel scared. They all did. He held Salma's hand to comfort her, and after a while she wiped her tears on her sleeve and stopped crying.

They came to a dark building set back from the road. It was the town jail. It was not part of the large fortress but a separate building where local people were imprisoned. When they came to the door the soldier laughed as though it had been a joke all along. He told the children they were free to go.

As they ran home Hani did not think it had been at all funny. He was angry that the soldier had upset Salma. He knew they would have to be careful and not give this soldier any excuse to make fun of them again. It also made him think about the prisoners he had seen arriving a few days before and how they must be suffering. What had just happened made him feel even closer to them, especially as he was still sure they were innocent.

He remembered the plaque and felt in his pocket to make sure it was still there.

8

Ninety-Nine Names

Later, when Hani was safely back home and the evening meal was over, he looked more carefully at the plaque they had found. It was beginning to rust in places but most of it was all right. He rubbed it with a few drops of olive oil hoping that would protect it for a bit longer and also help to show up the lettering.

His mother asked what he was doing. Oil was expensive and she did not want it wasted. He showed her the plaque and she looked at it with a puzzled expression on her face. She had never had the opportunity to learn to read so the tiny, faint words meant nothing to her.

"I've seen something similar, though," she said. "In the market. Some of them have verses from the Holy Qur'án engraved on them and people hang them in their houses."

Hani looked again at the lettering.

A Boy in 'Akká - 1868 to 1870

He could read Arabic but these words were written in a fancy way that made them difficult to make out. After studying them for a while longer he gave up and decided to discuss it with Baz the next day.

"I think that bit says 'King'," said Baz, pointing to one of the words and squinting in the hope of seeing it better.

The boys were sitting on the doorstep of Hani's house. Salma was nearby playing a game of five stones. She knew it was no good her trying to read anything as she had never been to school. Hani was teaching her the alphabet, though, and she was determined to be able to read one day. She was listening carefully to what the boys were saying.

Hani concentrated some more and found "Most Holy". Then he got stuck.

"My mother said they have plaques like these in the market," he told Baz. "Let's ask one of the metal-workers."

They raced each other along the lane, jumping over the smelly drain that ran down the middle and causing rats to leap in every direction. Salma trailed behind unable to keep up. Hani paused at the corner to look back to make sure she was still in sight. He knew it would not be safe if she were on her own when they reached the market. Dark, narrow passageways snaked off from the main street of the market and it was a dangerous place for girls as they were sometimes kidnapped. The three of them kept close together as they made their way between the crowded stalls where men and boys were selling everything from sticks of cinnamon to camel bells.

They heard the clink-clink of a metal-engraver at work and followed the sound until they discovered him sitting cross-legged on the ground working among piles of plaques and plates of  all shapes and sizes. Some of them had beautiful designs surrounding the quotations inscribed on them.

They watched him skilfully engrave the letters with a special chisel that made both thick and thin lines and fabulous swirls and flourishes.

A Boy in 'Akká - 1868 to 1870

"Are you wanting a plate?" he asked after a while.

"Not really," said Hani. "We just wondered if you could tell us what this means, please."

He held out the plaque and the man looked up briefly then back to his work. A few minutes passed before he finished the section he was working on and gave his full attention to the plaque.

"Yes, I know what this is," he said, after scrutinising it for a while. "But I have never made one." He traced his thin, sensitive fingers over the lettering.

"Where did you get it?" he asked.

"From the sea," said Baz.

"One of the words says 'Most Holy'," said Hani. "And we think another is 'King'."

"I can't read all the words," said the metal-engraver. "They are too faint. But it doesn't just say 'King', it says *Al-Malik* – The King."

He looked up and Hani was struck by the expression of deep devotion on the man's thin work-weary face.

"A person can be *a* king," he explained, "but *the*

King only refers to God. And it's the same with the other words – like *Al-Quddús*, The Most Holy."

He looked at the plaque again. *"Asmá' Alláh al-Husná,"* he whispered, "the 99 most beautiful Names of God."

He held the plaque reverently and began to recite some of the Names from memory in a sing-song voice that made Salma's head spin and she felt she was floating away.

"The Prophet Muhammad, peace be upon Him, said that anyone who memorizes them will enter Paradise," he told the children when he had finished.

"There's seems to be something in the centre as well," said Hani.

The metal-engraver hesitated, as though he knew something but did not want to say what it was.

"Too holy," he said at last, handing the plaque back to Hani.

Picking up the metal plate he had been working on, he continued with his engraving.

9

The Mysterious Letter in the Middle

Hani and Baz did not know who else to ask about the letter in the middle of the plaque. They asked Hani's father but all he could tell them was that there were indeed many Names of God throughout the Qur'án and the Traditions, and that 99 of them were called the Best of Names.

Then Yunus told them that God actually had 100 special Names, but nobody knew what the hundredth one was. It was hidden and called the Greatest Name.

Hani and Baz looked at each other in excitement. Could the middle letter be a clue to the hundredth Name? But it was impossible to see what it was.

The boys were wondering what to do next when Salma had an idea. She suggested they try to make a rubbing of the letter to see if that made it clearer to see. She found a thin scrap of paper and laid it over the engraving. Very carefully she began rubbing it with a piece of burnt charcoal while the boys pressed their fingers on the corners of the paper to stop it moving.

They watched as part of the letter slowly appeared.

"I think it's a B!" said Baz.

There were people called dervishes who lived in and around 'Akká. They lived simple lives and spent their days praying and meditating in the hope of getting closer to God. They did not work as others did but now and again came into town with their begging bowls and people would give them food.

A Boy in 'Akká - 1868 to 1870

They often promised to say a prayer in return and sometimes gave small tokens to people as a payment - usually holy words from the Qur'án written on a small piece of paper and folded in a scrap of cloth and tied with a bow, like a small parcel. These were treasured by people who could not read or write. They would often wear them on a ribbon round their necks to protect themselves, or else put them on a high shelf to bless their houses. Hani noticed that whenever a dervish came to the house his mother always gave him food, even when there was barely enough for themselves.

"Why don't they do any work?" he asked his father, who had instilled in him that it is important to work and no one should ever beg.

"Well, they think they should spend all their time trying to get close to God through praying and being detached from this world," Yunus explained.

"But how do they look after their children?" asked Hani, imagining babies dying of hunger if parents did not work.

"They don't usually marry," said Yunus.

He smiled. "It's just another way of living," he

explained, noticing Hani's worried expression. "I believe we should work as well as pray, and to marry and have children if it is meant to be. Some dervishes believe in magic and superstition, but others are very spiritual."

Hani looked thoughtful. If these people spent all their time praying and thinking about God, then perhaps they would know more about the mysterious letter B in the middle of the plaque? He decided that the next time a dervish came to the house for food he would ask him.

10

Trouble at School

Hani was in disgrace. He had asked a question that had angered the mullá who was teaching his class. Hani's crime had begun by asking how 'Alí, the holy son-in-law of the Prophet Muhammad, knew Muhammad was a Messenger from God when so many other people at the time did not.

To be fair, the mullá had tried to answer Hani's question. He said:

"Because it was obvious! Muhammad showed all the signs of a Messenger from God."

Hani's second question had also been answered, in part. He asked:

"What were the signs?"

And the mullá had explained about God speaking to Muhammad and giving Him a message to tell people.

Hani's third question began to cause the mullá to worry a little.

Trouble at School

"If it was obvious, why did some people not believe? And if He was a Messenger of God, why did they persecute Him and make Him suffer?"

The mullá had sighed.

"All of God's Messengers have suffered. People always rise up against them at first. It happened to Abraham and Jesus as well. Some people have prejudice in their hearts just because a Messenger of God comes in a way they don't expect. It is necessary to have a very pure heart to recognise a new Holy Messenger from God."

It was Hani's fourth question that had got him into trouble.

"If Messengers of God always suffer, could someone in our prison be One?"

Baz was sitting next to him and gave him a warning nudge with his elbow. The whole class stopped breathing as they watched their teacher's face turn deep purple under his turban.

Feeling very nervous, Hani added in a low voice, "It's just that Muhammad said the Holy Spirit would return on the Day of Resurrection."

He took a deep breath. "And Jesus said He would return. And the others," he added, his voice getting lower and lower as the teacher fixed him with an outraged eye. Hani knew there were others, like Krishna and Buddha and Zoroaster, because his father had told him.

"Perhaps," he ended in a whisper, "the new Holy One has come and the religious leaders have put Him in prison by mistake. How would we know?"

He was not quite sure what happened next, except that he was outside the room with his teacher holding him firmly by his ear and leading him to the chief mullá to be dealt with.

He was beaten with a stick five times on the soles of his feet and told not to return to school for a full month as he was a bad influence on the other children. And no-one was allowed to talk to him, not even his family.

11

A Good Question

Of course, Hani's family did talk to him. And so did Baz. But most other people murmured among themselves, saying it was not right for a child to say such things and that Hani had always asked difficult questions. His father was the same, they said, nodding as they remembered.

Hani's mother sighed when he hobbled home from school with bruised feet from the beating. She did not understand why he had to think so much about things. Why couldn't he leave the thinking to the mullás and be the same as other people? But secretly she was proud of him for being brave enough to ask his questions, and she gave him a hug.

"You must be careful," she told him. "People are always frightened of anything new. They think it means that the old is no longer true. Which isn't so, of course. Not always."

His father ruffled his hair and smiled.

A Boy in 'Akká - 1868 to 1870

"It was a good question, Hani," he said, a twinkle in his eye. "But your mother is right. Be careful."

He looked deep into Hani's eyes.

"And be careful where your heart is leading you. Remember to pray and ask God to guide you."

Hani thought about what his father had said. There was no way he wanted to do anything that was displeasing to God. In fact, he already felt that God was guiding him, otherwise why was he feeling so excited and be given so many clues to follow?

Hani did not normally have much spare time during the week as mornings were taken up with school, which lasted from seven until noon. During this time he sat on a rush mat on the floor with sixty other boys learning the Qur'án by heart and doing writing exercises. The mullás were very strict and used to hit boys who fell asleep as they rocked back and forth chanting the verses hour after hour. And, as Hani had learnt, questions were not always welcome!

Then, in the afternoons, he usually had to help his father in the workshop until evening, although sometimes he finished early if his father was not

A Good Question

busy. The only other time he had free was on Fridays, which was a day when nobody worked. Apart from going to the mosque for an hour in the morning to pray and hear the weekly sermon, the rest of the day was spent visiting friends and relatives. It was also a time when people ventured outside the city walls to have picnics in the fields, which were covered in beautiful red flowers, especially in spring.

Not having to go to school gave Hani more time to spend on his search.

12

The Pilgrim on the Wall

Hani was watching the fortress from the shelter of a square look-out post built into the wide, outer wall of the city. It was here he had seen several strangers standing for hours looking hopefully towards the prison. You needed sharp eyes to see anything from that distance and Hani was curious to know what they were trying to see.

The look-out post was also a favourite place for soldiers to rest when patrolling the wall, and Hani was hoping that none would turn up while he was there.

The sun beat down and Hani sat in the shade with his back against a wall. He had been there for a couple of hours, waiting.

The Pilgrim on the Wall

With a start, he opened his eyes. He must have dozed off.

He heard muffled voices. Soldiers? He peered cautiously over the top of the wall and breathed a sigh of relief. Two strangers were walking up the steps, whispering excitedly. They were dressed differently from the local people and were wearing small turbans on their heads instead of fezzes. Hani could not understand everything they were saying, although some of the words were familiar. He did not know it at the time but the men were speaking Farsi, the language of Persia.

The first of the men reached the top and was so busy talking to his companion that he did not notice Hani. But the second man did, and he made a sign to the first man to stop speaking. They seemed very nervous. Hani was hoping to ask them some questions, but to his disappointment they quickly went back down the steps and hurried away. He guessed they were secret followers of the Leader of the band of prisoners.

"They must have thought I was a spy or something," sighed Hani, wishing he knew what had made them travel thousands of miles from their own country to see the Prisoner. They must love Him very much, he decided.

It was then that he saw an old man further along the wall. The man seemed to be in a trance and was gazing at the fortress. Around his neck hung a tray of needles, thimbles and other trinkets for  sale. Hani noticed that they were rusty from being exposed to the salty spray from the sea and could not imagine anyone wanting to buy them. The man was looking intently at a window in the fortress, screwing up his eyes in an effort to see. Hani turned his head to also look. And his heart began to beat faster as he clearly saw a handkerchief being waved from an upper window.

But the look of joy on the old man's face began to fade as, try as he might, he could not see anything. His eyesight was too weak, and while he could make out the large shadow of the fortress, it was impossible for him to see if anyone was waving.

The Pilgrim on the Wall

After standing a while longer, he began to weep with disappointment, and Hani felt his own eyes welling up in sympathy.

Unseen by either Hani or the old man, members of the Prisoner's family were watching from the fortress, and they too were in tears. They had noticed the old man standing on the wall day after day and knew he had walked all the way from the cave where he lived on Mount Carmel, fourteen miles around the bay.

The Prisoner's heart was full of love for this dear follower of His, and He prayed that something would happen to allow all the pilgrims to freely come into His presence.

The man calmed down, as though he felt the love of the Prisoner reaching his heart. And he chanted the most beautiful prayer Hani had ever heard. As he listened, Hani had a feeling of deepest peace.

Later, as he walked home, he remembered some of the words of the prayer and tried to chant them the way the old man had done. He felt he was floating as light as a feather and that his feet were barely touching the ground.

He passed a group of his friends, not fellow students who were still forbidden to speak to him but some of the street children who were allowed to run wild. They called to him to come and join them in jumping off the wall into the sea, but this time he just smiled and shook his head.

He did not want anything to break the spell of indescribable happiness he was feeling.

13

The Dervish at the Door

One day Hani heard a soft knock at the door of his house.

Outside was a young man with long hair and a scraggly beard and wearing a small, dusty, embroidered cap and an even dustier earth-coloured cloak.

He was a dervish, and he was holding a small wooden bowl which Hani's mother silently filled with bread from that morning's baking. The man murmured a blessing and was so hungry he sat down on his heels in the road to eat it.

A Boy in 'Akká - 1868 to 1870

Hani had been waiting for an opportunity to talk to a dervish ever since his father had told him that they spend their time praying to God to find the truth about things. He waited until the young man had finished eating the bread and then crouched down beside him.

Hani took the plaque from his pocket and showed it to the dervish, who lifted it to his lips and kissed it. He seemed to know what it was but said he could not read very well. However, he said he knew another dervish who could.

He wanted to keep the plaque, but Hani said no, quite sure he would never see it again.

"Where is this person?" asked Hani.

The dervish shrugged and vaguely waved his hand over his shoulder.

"Can you show me?"

The dervish nodded and got to his feet, and Hani quickly called out to his mother to tell her what he was going to do.

Before she had a chance to say anything, he was off down the lane after the dervish, who was walking rapidly away. Hani had not gone far when

The Dervish at the Door

he heard running footsteps behind him and looked round to see his fifteen-year-old brother trying to catch up with him. His mother had been worried seeing Hani going off on his own and had called her older son to go with him. Fuad was always teasing him and Hani hoped he would not make fun of him now or spoil this chance of finding something important.

14

A Mysterious Answer

Hani came to the Land Gate, which was set in the strong wall that had originally been built to protect the city. He passed some sleepy soldiers who were supposed to check who was coming and going and to report on anything suspicious.

The soldiers took no notice of a poor dervish passing through the gate followed by a youth and a boy, and half an hour later Hani found himself in a field where an elderly dervish was praying by a stream.

While Hani waited for the older dervish to speak, the younger one went to the far end of the field,

A Mysterious Answer

and lighting a small fire of twigs, boiled a mixture of wild leaves and water to make tea. Fuad was not interested in deciphering the plaque and wandered off to join him.

Eventually the elderly dervish opened his eyes and looked enquiringly at Hani, who showed him the plaque and explained that he thought the middle letter was B but did not know what it meant.

The dervish seemed very interested. He explained that there were many prophecies about it.

"This letter in the centre represents the Greatest Name of God," he said. "People pray to find it. And that is what I am doing."

A Boy in 'Akká - 1868 to 1870

He looked searchingly at Hani, his eyes seeming to burn into his soul.

"There is nothing greater than the Glory of God," he said. "And there is nothing more to be said."

Then he shut his eyes and began meditating again.

Hani felt a thrill pass through him at the dervish's words, but he was also mystified. He longed to ask him what he meant but felt it would be rude to interrupt. It was obviously time to leave. He looked around for Fuad, but he was fast asleep in a corner of the field.

Fuad arrived home several hours after Hani. He was groaning and holding his head, saying it felt as though a herd of wild camels was galloping around inside it.

"It was the tea!" he moaned, when his mother asked him what was wrong. "The leaves must have been some kind of drug and I didn't know!"

"There I was thinking Hani needed to be looked after," said Pari crossly, "and really it was you! You should never eat or drink anything unless you know what it is!" she scolded. "And only then if you know it is right!"

A Mysterious Answer

She sighed. She had been worried when her sons had gone off with the dervish and was relieved when they returned home safely, even if Fuad was suffering from a sore head. But she still felt uncomfortable with all the questions her younger son was asking and felt in her bones that it would only lead to trouble. Already Hani had caused the displeasure of that soldier who was patrolling the wall, then he had been excluded from school, and now he had been mixed up with dervishes. Where would it all end?

But Hani knew that what he felt in his heart was very real and that he was being led closer and closer to knowing God's Greatest Name. He was not going to give up now!

He wondered what the older dervish had meant when he said that there was nothing greater than the Glory of God. Was that another clue?

15

Collecting Clues

Yunus had never told Hani about the prophecies to do with the greatness of 'Akká. He was as worried as his wife about the situations his young son kept finding himself in and did not want to add to them by making him even keener to solve the spiritual riddle of the hundredth Name.

He decided to keep Hani busy by involving him more in his carpentry business; it was time he learnt more skills than just putting on handles and polishing the finished coffins. Last time there had been an outbreak of cholera Yunus had not been able to make coffins quickly enough for all the people who had died. Fuad used to help him but was now building boats with one of his uncles. It would be good to have Hani's help to get a stock ready ahead of time before the next outbreak.

When Hani was told he did not mind. As he worked he was free to think. Baz had recently painted the

Collecting Clues

tin box that had contained the plaque and it was now white with a pattern of leaves showing through and looked really nice. He and Baz had decided to put all the clues they had found in the box, but so far there was only one and that was the plaque itself.

All the other clues were in their heads – the metal-worker telling them that the words were the 99 Names or Attributes of God; Salma discovering it was the letter B in the middle; the old dervish saying something about the Glory of God; the smell of roses when the prisoners had come ashore; the lovely feeling when Hani heard one of the followers chanting a prayer; and strangers standing on the city wall hoping to see the Prisoner's hand waving from the window. (Hani had decided long ago to think of the Prisoner with a capital P.) And, of course, those strange lights in the sky.

"Careful," said his father as Hani shaved too much off the lid of a coffin with a chisel. "It needs to fit tightly."

Hani tried to concentrate.

A Boy in 'Akká - 1868 to 1870

Yunus went back to his own work and his own thoughts. He remembered hearing that all the prisoners had fallen ill shortly after they had arrived in the prison, and that three of them died. Two of them were brothers who died with their arms around each other. Yunus had expected the prison authorities to order three coffins, but no order came.

A guard told him later that the Leader of the new group of prisoners had no belongings except a small rug, which was the only thing He had to sleep on. He gave the rug to the soldiers to sell to pay for a proper burial for the men; but when the soldiers sold it, they kept the money for themselves. Yunus had been very upset when he heard about it.

"Never mind," he said out loud as he was remembering these things. "Now they are in the next world all their troubles are over."

Hani look up, but his father seemed to be talking to himself.

Hani had always thought it was a bit morbid making coffins, but thinking more deeply about it he realised it was really quite a nice thing to do. At the same time as someone's body died, their soul went on to the next world. It was a very spiritual time.

And, thought Hani as he admired a pattern his father was carving on one of the more expensive coffins, making a coffin as best as you could showed respect for a body that had been connected to a soul all of its life.

16

Delivering Bread

Baz burst into the workroom as Hani was on his own sweeping up at the end of the day.

"You'll never guess!" he said.

"What?"

"I've got to deliver the bread to the fortress tomorrow!"

Baz hopped from one foot to the other in excitement. His father was a baker and delivered bread all over the town but had never allowed Baz to do the delivery to the prison.

"Can you come with me? We might be able to see inside!"

Hani's face broke into a smile. He had been thinking they had come to a dead end in their search.

"What time do we need to go?" he asked.

Delivering Bread

"About five tomorrow morning," said Baz. "Can you come?"

Hani was sure his parents would say yes.

"I'll meet you at your house," he said.

At dawn the following day there were already a number of people in the streets. Tradesmen balanced flat boards on their heads heaped with cheese and dates and freshly baked bread, while others skilfully carried trays of small cups of hot sweet tea without spilling a drop. Their calls could be heard up and down the lanes. Doors opened as they passed, and servants reached out to buy what the households needed for breakfast.

There were Muslim men hurrying to the mosques to pray, black-hatted Jews on their way to the synagogue, and Christians going to church for early morning service.

There were also beggar-children sleeping on the streets, and Hani's heart hurt when he saw them.

The bread for the prison was too heavy to carry on their heads, so Baz was using a cart which he and Hani pulled along behind them. The wheels were made of iron and bounced noisily over the cobbled streets and several loaves at the bottom became broken. Hani and Baz give it to the children, hoping no one at the prison would notice if the order was a few loaves short.

"They probably wouldn't want to pay for the broken bread anyway," said Baz.

They soon left the busy part of town and struggled up a deserted road by the sea until they came to the entrance of the fortress.

Baz explained to the guard outside that his father had asked him to deliver the bread, and the man lifted the cloth to inspect what was underneath. He gave the boys a searching look, then opened

Delivering Bread

the gate and signalled for them to go in. They walked up the path, where three soldiers were leaning on their rifles. The soldiers glanced briefly at the boys as they passed but did not try to stop them; they had been on duty all night and were tired and longing for their beds. Hani noticed some old cannon balls lying in the grass and a cannon facing out to sea.

The fortress loomed large and menacing and its dark shadow fell on the boys. Close to, it was much bigger than Hani had realised. He looked up to see if any prisoner was looking out of the barred windows, but there was no one there.

They came to an outbuilding and a cook from the kitchen came running out, shouting at them to hurry.

"You're late!" he growled, beginning to unload the bread.

"It's my father's best bread," said Baz with a smile. He knew there were different grades of bread, some made with better flour than others. He had been pleased at the thought that such good bread was going to feed the prisoners.

"I should hope so," said the cook. "This is for the soldiers, not the prisoners!"

He laughed and pointed to a wooden box in a corner.

"That's for the prisoners!"

Baz and Hani looked at the box in dismay. It was full of black bread that looked as though it had been mixed with mud.

"But doesn't it make them ill?" protested Hani.

The cook gave him a sharp look.

"So what?" he said, and frowned at Hani, who was still staring at the dirty bread. "Are you sympathising with the prisoners?" he asked suspiciously.

Delivering Bread

"Are they very dangerous?" interrupted Baz quickly, rescuing Hani so he would not have to answer "yes" and get into trouble. "We heard the last lot are."

The cook hesitated. What happened in the prison was supposed to be confidential but he did like a bit of gossip.

"Here. Help me get all this bread out of the cart and into the kitchen," he said, gathering another armful.

As they walked back and forth in and out of the kitchen, the cook said the staff had been told that the last lot of prisoners were the worst you could find and had been accused of trying to overthrow the religion of Islam itself.

"But I think someone got it wrong," he said. "They are the gentlest folk ever. And they never complain, except they did happen to mention politely that the black bread was so full of salt the children had difficulty eating it. There are babies with them too, you see. So the governor said one of them could go with a guard to the market to exchange three of the black loaves for two better ones. Then later he said they could have the money instead and buy their own. It's just a few pence, mind, which doesn't buy much, 'specially for seventy of them. Never heard of that being allowed before."

He rubbed his chin thoughtfully.

"It's the son who usually goes," he added. "Everyone loves him and his Father."

He emptied the cart of the last of the bread and stood for a moment lost in thought, completely forgetting the number of loaves he should have been counting.

"What's His name?" asked Hani, trying not to sound too curious. "The Father's," he added casually, taking care not to look at the cook as he spoke and busying himself with arranging the last flat loaf neatly on top of the others.

He felt the cook's eyes looking at him and gave a yawn, pretending he was not really interested in knowing.

The cook grunted. "I don't know for sure," he said, "but I think I heard someone say it was Husayn Alí."

Hani hid his disappointment. It did not begin with B. But still, he thought, there was obviously something very special about the Prisoner and even the cook had noticed it.

Delivering Bread

As he and Baz made their way back to the gate, one of the sleepy soldiers took a closer look at them. It was the soldier who had frightened them when they had been fishing and found the box with the plaque.

He shot his rifle into the air and said something that made the other soldiers laugh.

"*Run!*" he shouted.

As the boys fled down the rest of the path, a soft white feather floated down from a bird flying high overhead and landed in the cart. Then the boys shot through the gate to safety.

17

The Free Bird

Hani and Baz waited for a moment to get their breath back.

"I thought he was going to shoot us this time!" said Baz.

Hani was also shaken. "He wouldn't dare do that," he said. "But he is a bully."

As they walked back to Baz's house, Hani wanted to forget about the soldier and think of happier things.

"I told you those prisoners were different," he said. "Even the cook says so."

Baz looked thoughtful. "You know he said the Prisoner's son is allowed out with a guard to exchange the bread? Well, if we knew when they went, we could follow them."

The Free Bird

"We could watch from the wall opposite," suggested Hani.

It was then that he noticed the feather in the cart.

"That should go in our box," he said. "It's another sign. Fancy that bird flying over at that exact moment."

Hani was showing Salma the feather and she was feeling its silky softness between her fingers as he was telling her about his visit to the prison. He left out the bit about the soldier but her eyes still filled with tears.

"What's wrong?" asked Hani, wondering what had upset her.

"I was thinking," said Salma, "about that bird flying free in the sky. And how those poor prisoners are shut up in cells. Like birds shut in cages and not able to fly anymore."

Her mother came over and gave her a hug.

"There are many things that are not fair in this world," she said. "And if those prisoners haven't done anything wrong, then God will make it all right in the end."

"But what if they die?" asked Salma.

"Then God will make it right in the next world," said Pari.

"Why doesn't God punish the people who put them in prison?" Salma insisted, thinking that was not fair either. "I hate those guards!"

Pari turned to stir a pot of soup on the fire.

"The guards just have to do what they are told," she said, putting a handful of herbs in the pot.

She knew that sometimes wrong decisions were made because of prejudice or fear and that these often came from some of the religious leaders, who were very powerful at the time. Even the kings had to do what they said. But she knew there were some good religious leaders too and did not want Salma to think they were all bad.

"The cook said the guards like the new prisoners," said Hani, to comfort his sister. "So I expect they are being as kind to them as they can be."

18

A Hand at the Window

What Hani said was true. Several of the guards had come to love the new prisoners and were as puzzled as Hani why they had been sent as criminals to 'Akká.

Hani knew that conditions in the fortress were very hard because a boy at school, whose uncle was a policeman, had told him. There were no beds or blankets, and in winter it was damp and cold. There was no glass in the windows, just bars, which did not keep out the cold wind blowing off the sea. And in summer it was like an oven. There was never enough to eat and the prisoners were often ill.

He wished he and Baz could take fresh food to the prison the next time they went. But how would they know it would be given to them and not eaten by the guards? It would be impossible to know.

Meanwhile, he decided to keep watch on the wall for when the Prisoner's son left with a guard to buy bread.

Days passed, but neither Hani nor Baz caught sight of any prisoner leaving the fortress. They did not realise that a back entrance to the prison was probably being used, one that led to a narrow lane near a busy market. However, their time was not wasted because something interesting happened.

One day they saw a traveller on the beach washing his clothes in the sea and laying them out on the rocks to dry. The man had once been rich but now was so poor he did not even have a change of clothes to wear. He had walked for six months from Persia to reach 'Akká and arrived exhausted and covered in dust. He slept while the sun dried his clothes, and then he put them on again.

A Hand at the Window

The boys could not help smiling. The man's trousers and shirt had shrunk and he did look funny. He stood looking down at his too-small clothes in despair. But at least they were now clean, even if they had shrunk. He said a prayer, then began to walk round the fortress.

Hani and Baz watched as he circled the fortress. He seemed to be praying and crying at the same time. Then they saw him look up to the top window. They looked up as well. And there was a hand beckoning the pilgrim to come in! The man went to the main gate and passed the guards, who did not make any attempt to stop him, and disappeared inside.

When he did not reappear the boys hoped he had managed to reach the Prisoner. Either that or he had been imprisoned himself. But it looked as though the guards at the gate just had not seen him – as though God had veiled their eyes as he passed by.

It was not until several days later that Hani and Baz saw him again. He was walking through the town and had a peaceful smile on his face. Hani ran to speak to him and ask what had happened when he had gone into the prison, but the man's thoughts were in another world and he did not even hear him. He vanished down the street and they never saw him again, although they searched in the lanes for a long time afterwards.

19

Spies and Another Clue

Hani and Baz were walking near the Land Gate that led into the town when they heard a great commotion. Soldiers sprang towards a man who was entering the town and threw him to the ground. They took his bundle of belongings then pushed him back out of the gate, threatening him with their guns and forbidding him to return. Hani heard laughter above his head and glanced up to see two men looking very pleased with themselves at the window of a small room above the gate.

"Spies," whispered an old man in the crowd, jerking his head to indicate he was talking about the two men laughing above.

Hani made his way towards the old man and whispered back, "Spies?"

The man nodded and began to hurry away. Hani followed, leaving Baz behind still staring after the

Spies and Another Clue

unfortunate traveller as he limped away from the town.

"Why spies?" Hani asked the old man.

The man hesitated. He looked around to make sure no one could overhear him.

"They tell the soldiers if any stranger is coming into the town," he explained, "especially anyone trying to see the Prisoner."

A Boy in 'Akká - 1868 to 1870

Hani's heart beat faster. The man had said "the" Prisoner, and as the prison was full of hundreds of prisoners, he must mean the special one.

"Why would they want to see Him?" he asked. "Why is He special?"

"Haven't you heard?" said the man in surprise. "People say He is the Expected One from God."

Hani held his breath for several seconds before letting it out in a long sigh. At last he was finding something more about the mysterious Prisoner!

"But why have they put Him in prison?" he asked.

The man suddenly became nervous and refused to say anything more.

"Please," begged Hani. "I really want to know. And I'm not a spy!" he added desperately.

"I can't tell you any more," said the man, walking quickly into a courtyard and up some stone steps to a cell-like room where travellers stayed.

Hani stood at the bottom of the steps, feeling it would be rude to follow.

Baz appeared beside him and Hani told him what the man had said.

Spies and Another Clue

"I heard something too," said Baz. "The Prisoner claims to have a new Message from God that will unite the world."

"Is that why they have put Him in prison?" asked Hani in surprise.

Baz nodded. "Don't you remember what our teacher said the day you were asking all those questions? He said that people always oppose a Messenger of God when He comes at first. Look how they treated Muhammad. And Jesus."

Hani remembered the conversation well and how much trouble it had got him into. That had all happened a month ago when he had been suspended from school. He was due back the next day.

"Come on," he said to Baz, realising it was getting late and his mother would be worried. "Let's go. Now we know where this old man lives we can come back another day and perhaps he will tell us more."

20

Hani in Jail

Hani never did get to school next day. He was on his way, a slate for writing under his arm and his lunch of bread and cheese in his pocket, when he suddenly felt a hand on the back of his collar and he was roughly pulled backwards.

His slate crashed to the ground and shattered into pieces.

Twisting his head, Hani came face to face with the soldier the children had met the day they found the plaque, and who later had frightened him and Baz  in the prison when they were delivering bread.

"Now I've found you out!" growled the soldier, looking pleased with himself. "I saw you!"

Hani in Jail

Hani had no idea what he meant but was unable to say anything because the soldier was twisting the collar of his shirt and he could hardly breathe.

"Stealing!" said the soldier triumphantly.

Hani almost choked in surprise. Stealing? He had never stolen anything in his life!

He was dragged to the police station where the soldier announced that he had seen Hani stealing a valuable bracelet from one of the stalls.

Hani protested that he was innocent but nobody took any notice. He was taken to the town jail, pushed into a cell, and the door was locked behind him.

He looked around and found the cell was crowded with other small boys ranging in age from five to twelve. They were all unwashed and seemed to be starving. They began searching his pockets and fought over who would eat the bread and cheese.

Hani did not know what to do. He felt helpless. How could he get a message to his father to let him know what was happening? Who would believe his word against that of the soldier? And why was the soldier doing this to him?

A Boy in 'Akká - 1868 to 1870

Through the high-up barred window of the cell he heard the Call to Prayer that was announced five times a day from the mosque to remind everyone to say their prayers. He had nowhere to wash but found a corner in the cell to perform his prayer. A couple of other boys did the same. The rest sat listlessly staring in front of them with blank expressions on their faces. Hani wondered how long they had been there and if some of them too had been wrongly accused.

He turned his heart to God and asked for His help.

❁❁❁

Baz was frantic with worry. Not only did Hani not turn up for school, but when Baz went to his house afterwards to see if he was there, his parents did not know where he was either. They began to check up on his friends to see if he was with them, while Baz searched along the wall near the fortress.

Hani in Jail

Then one of the street boys said he had seen a soldier take Hani to the town jail. Baz ran through the streets as fast as he could to tell Hani's parents.

Yunus went to the highest police authorities several times to protest his son's innocence. No bracelet had been found on Hani but no one seemed bothered about that. They said he could have thrown it away when he was caught. They called the owner of the stall to the jail to identify the thief, but he stood scratching his head, not sure if Hani was the boy or not as he had only seen the back of him. The soldier who had arrested him insisted he was the one, so he was kept in jail.

When Hani woke up on the first morning he found his shoes had been stolen. And when the once-a-day meal of watery soup with a chunk of black bread arrived, he had to fight to get his share before the bigger boys ate it all.

The one thing Hani found helped get through the nightmare of those days was saying his prayers. Not only did he say the daily Muslim prayers, but he also asked the mysterious Prisoner in the fortress to help him.

A Boy in 'Akká - 1868 to 1870

One day as Hani was praying, his brother happened to be in the market when he saw a boy trying to sell a bracelet to a passer-by. The man was beginning to look suspicious and the boy suddenly turned and ran away. Fuad raced after him, but the boy was weaving in and out of the crowd and soon disappeared.

Fuad was wondering which way to go when he noticed something move under one of the stalls, and when he bent down to look, the boy shot out and made off again. Fuad leapt over a box of cactus fruit and caught him just before he vanished in a labyrinth of lanes. The boy was still holding the bracelet, and with Fuad glaring at him, soon admitted it was the one Hani had been accused of stealing several days before.

The police returned it to the shopkeeper; and when the soldier who had arrested Hani was told he just shrugged and said he must have made a mistake because the boys looked the same. Fuad did not say anything, but he knew this was not true because the boy did not look anything like Hani.

Hani was freed, but those few days in jail had been very frightening and he never forgot them. He now knew what it was like to be imprisoned when you were innocent and how lonely and helpless it made you feel.

When he returned home he was more determined than ever to continue his search. There were so many unjust and unhappy things happening in the world, and he was sure that the Prisoner had the power to make things right.

21

The Master in the Market

"I think you will become a mullá when you grow up!" laughed Pari when she had her son safely home again and he told her how much the prayers had helped him in the jail.

Hani did not think so. He did not want to be a mullá. But he did have a feeling that God was trying to tell him something important. Otherwise, why would he have had that vision about banners of light and known they had something to do with the Prisoner? And why had he felt so close to the Prisoner when he was in the jail?

One result of the jail episode was that his teacher at school was kinder to him. And he became a bit of a hero among the other boys. Not that that mattered to Hani; he was much more interested in getting to the bottom of the mystery and finding out why it was filling him with such excitement. He had never had such a feeling before.

The Master in the Market

It was then that Hani saw him! Not the Prisoner, but the Prisoner's son. He was walking towards the market with two guards, one on either side of him. Long chains were locked around his wrists and clanked as he walked along. But his head was held high and the guards were very respectful as they walked beside him.

Hani knew at once who he was. He recognised him from that first time he had seen him helping people ashore from the boat. He must, thought Hani, be going to buy bread for the rest of the prisoners.

A group of street boys noisily followed the handsome young man, and many people stopped to stare. There was something so dynamic yet calm about him that Hani could not turn his eyes away. The guards kept tucking the young man's chains beneath his cloak so people would not see them, but when they fell down again he did not seem to mind. He had a very kind expression on his face.

"I hear people call him the Master," said one of the shopkeepers, who had left his shop and was standing next to Hani.

Hani turned to ask what else he had heard, but the man had already gone back to his shop to serve a customer.

Hani's eyes followed the Master until he was out of sight. He remained standing, gazing at the spot where he had last seen him, for a long time afterwards.

22

Telling Salma

Feeling as though he was in some kind of a trance, Hani went to Baz's house to tell him what he had seen, but Baz was busy helping his father and could not listen at that moment.

"I'll come over later," said Baz, busy piling bread into the cart ready to be taken to the market.

So Hani told Salma instead. She was playing with a doll her father had carved out of a left-over piece of wood. The doll had moveable wooden joints and was so cleverly made all Salma's friends wanted her father to make one for them as well. Yunus had grumbled that making dolls would not pay the bills, but he had a soft heart and promised he would when he had some spare time.

Hani duly admired his sister's doll, and then he told her about the prisoner he had seen in the town. Salma could not understand why her brother

was so excited and continued to plait the doll's long woollen hair.

"He was somehow different,' said Hani, trying to explain. 'He stood out in the crowd."

"He must have been very tall, then," said Salma, wrapping a colourful piece of material around the doll and trying to make it look like a dress.

"Not really," said Hani, surprised when he thought about it. "No taller than most people there."

"Then how did he stand out?" asked Salma, suddenly interested.

"He sort of ... shone!" replied Hani eventually.

Salma gazed at him wide-eyed. "Like a lamp?" she asked.

"No," said Hani, struggling for words. "It was like an invisible light."

"Then how did you see it?" asked Salma. To her, if you could not actually see something then it was not there.

"I suppose I felt it," said Hani. "And not just me," he added quickly, seeing Salma opening her mouth to object again. "Lots of people couldn't stop looking at him. Even the shopkeepers came out to look. It was a very warm feeling," he added.

"Oh," said Salma, tying a small triangle of material round the head of her doll. "Like I know mummy loves me even when she doesn't say it."

"Like a *million* mothers," said Hani.

23

Remembering

Hani had just finished telling Baz for the third time about seeing the Master. Baz had made him repeat the story over and over again in case he had left anything out.

They decided to examine the contents of their box again, but it still did not have anything in it apart from the plaque and the feather.

"Do you remember going to the fortress?" Baz asked, looking at the feather with a rueful smile. "And how that soldier fired his gun in the air to frighten us?"

Hani pulled a face, thinking how the same soldier had ordered them off the beach and later had him imprisoned.

"But we also learned from the cook how everyone loves the Prisoner and His family," he said.

"We haven't thought about the clues we've found since then," said Baz. "Like that man. You know, the one who washed his clothes and they shrunk, and then he went into the prison."

"Yes, and he was in there for ages and when we saw him later he looked as though he had been in heaven!" said Hani. "Something very special must have happened there to make him so happy. He must have seen the Prisoner."

"And God made the guards not see him," added Baz with a chuckle. "So they didn't stop him! It was as though he was invisible!"

The boys were quiet as they thought what it must have been like to walk passed the guards like that, right into the prison and into the presence of the Prisoner.

"Then there was that man who told you about the spies who live above the Land Gate. The ones who stop the followers of the Prisoner being allowed in," said Baz, breaking the silence. "And how he said the Prisoner is the Expected One from God."

"I sort of guessed that," said Hani. "From the

Remembering

beginning. It got me in a lot of trouble at school!" he reminded Baz.

"And then yesterday you saw the Prisoner's son again," said Baz.

"And had the same good feeling as the first time," said Hani. "And not just me but other people there."

"If he is called the Master, imagine how wonderful his Father must be," said Baz. "An actual Messenger of God."

The boys sighed and picked up the plaque to have a look at it again. They were still puzzled by the letter B in the middle of the 99 Names of God.

"The engraver in the market said the meaning of that letter is very holy," said Baz.

"And the dervish said we have to pray to find it," said Hani, suddenly remembering.

They shut their eyes and Baz said a prayer.

"Let's visit that man who said the Prisoner is the Expected One," suggested Hani when they had finished.

They ran to the courtyard where Hani had last seen him and up the steps to the room, but it was empty and it seemed no one was living there anymore.

The boys turned away, disappointed.

"But we mustn't give up," said Hani.

24

A Change of Heart

Hani was in the market, having been sent by his mother to buy spices. It was stifling hot and he was struggling against a crowd of people coming in while he was trying to get out.

He found himself squashed between two fat men. They did not take any notice of him, and he could not have moved anyway as his arms were pinned to his sides. The noise of the market around him faded to a hum as his head became engulfed in the folds of their robes.

"It's the talk of the prison," said one of the men.

A Change of Heart

Hani pricked up his ears.

"There was this person, a learned shaykh or something, well-known in the town," said the man. "Well, he came to the gate of the prison and demanded to see this Prisoner - you know, the one I told you about who is the leader of the group from Persia. Seeing as how the shaykh was important, the guards let him in. I'd had a few days off," he added, "but everyone was talking about it when I returned."

He paused and his friend and Hani waited to hear what happened next.

"They told the shaykh to wait while one of them went to the Prisoner's cell to ask if He wanted to see him or not. And do you know what the Prisoner said?"

"I wouldn't have thought He had a choice whether to say yes or no!" said his friend scornfully. "He was just a prisoner after all!"

The first man did not reply. What his friend said would normally be true, but most of the guards loved this Prisoner and treated Him with respect. However, he knew that if he said this, his friend would not understand.

"Well, anyway," he said, "the Prisoner sent a message back saying that the shaykh could come – but only if he got rid of the dagger he was hiding under his cloak!"

"But," spluttered the second man, his mouth dropping open in astonishment, "how did He know it was there?"

Hani was also astonished. He disentangled his head from the robes and took a gulp of much-needed air.

"Even the guards didn't know!" said the first man. "Apparently the shaykh had planned to kill the Prisoner. And there's more," he added, lowering his voice so Hani had to stretch his neck to hear. "The shaykh came back a few days later. He was searched, and as he didn't have the dagger on him, the Prisoner was asked if it would be all right to bring him up this time."

"And did He agree?"

The first man gave a chuckle. "No. He said to tell the shaykh to first get rid of the hatred in his heart and then he could come!"

The men looked at each other over the top of Hani's head, wonderment written all over their faces.

A Change of Heart

"When the shaykh was given this message he went as white as a ghost, for it seems his heart *was* full of hatred," continued the first man. "He had secretly decided to kill the Prisoner with his bare hands! He hurried away and no one thought he would ever come back. But he did."

"And?" asked the second man.

"This time the Prisoner agreed to see him!"

"But was it safe?" Although he knew nothing about the Prisoner, the second man suddenly could not bear the thought of Him being hurt. Hani was also worried.

The first man nodded. "When the shaykh was taken to the prison cell, he fell to his knees and wept and begged the Prisoner to forgive him! I tell you, this Prisoner is not like you or me. He has the power to change people's hearts."

Hani felt his own heart quicken within him. He pulled his hands free with a jerk and some of the spices in the bag he was carrying flew out and made him sneeze. The two men looked down in surprise, having forgotten he was there. At that moment the people around them began to move and Hani managed to wriggle through the crowd and out of the market.

As he ran home he thought his heart would jump out of his mouth with excitement.

"That's beautiful!" said Hani's mother when he told her what he had overheard. "What a happy world it would be if all the hatred in people's hearts was turned to love like that."

And she decided not to scold Hani for being late and for losing half the spices as he ran home.

"But how did the Prisoner know?' she asked. 'About the dagger and what the shaykh was thinking?"

"I don't know," said Hani. "But I think He just knows everything."

25

The Sacrifice
(June 1870)

Two years had passed since Hani and Baz first began their search. Although they had discovered some wonderful things about the Prisoner, they were still baffled by the mystery of the hundredth Name. And it had been a long time since they had found anything new.

Then, in the summer of 1870, Hani's father heard that another person had died in the prison. It was the Prisoner's son.

"Not the Master!" Hani cried out in dismay when his father told him.

"No," said Yunus. "It's another son. A younger one. His name was Mihdí. People say there was something very special about him too. They say he was very gentle and everyone loved him. He was only twenty-two years old," he ended sadly.

"How did he die?" asked Hani, thinking that

A Boy in 'Akká - 1868 to 1870

perhaps one of the guards had shot him.

"I heard he was saying prayers," said Yunus. "On the flat roof of the prison. And that he was so carried away by his love of God that he forgot about an open skylight in the roof and fell through to the room below."

Yunus had also heard that the Prisoner had offered to heal His son, even though a doctor had said he was so badly injured there was no hope of saving his life. But Mihdí had said he wished to die as a sacrifice so that people would be allowed to come into the presence of his beloved Father and not just have to stand on the wall outside hoping to see a glimpse of His hand waving through the prison window.

Yunus waited for an order to come from the prison authorities asking him for a coffin, but none came. He hoped that whoever they asked did a good job. If I had been asked, he thought, I would have given them the best and most beautiful coffin I had.

As the coffin was being lowered into the grave, a gentle earthquake shook the ground. Everyone felt it for miles around. It was as though the earth itself was opening its arms to welcome the Prisoner's son, thought Yunus.

26

The Missing Clue

Just four months after the death of Mihdí, part of the fortress was needed to house a regiment of soldiers. The Prisoner and His family were taken to live in a house nearby, where they had a little more freedom but were still not allowed to leave the city.

However, this did mean that it was easier for the Prisoner's followers to visit him, if they managed first of all to get through the gate where spies were still watching in order to report them to the authorities.

So, thought Yunus to himself, the dying wish of Mihdí, that people could more freely visit his Father, was coming true. And he decided to tell Hani about the prophecies mentioning 'Akká he had tried to discuss with the mullá two years earlier.

When Hani heard about the prophecies, his interest immediately flared up again.

A Boy in 'Akká - 1868 to 1870

"Do they really say that the person who visits 'Akká is blessed by God?" he asked in awe.

Yunus nodded. "And the Prophet Muhammad said that whoever visits the visitor of 'Akká will be especially blessed."

"The Visitor could mean the Prisoner!" exclaimed Hani. "And pilgrims visiting Him. I wish I knew more about Him."

Yunus looked at his son thoughtfully.

"I have known for some time," he admitted. "But it was too dangerous to tell you. There are some of His followers living in the caravanserai in the town. The one near the mosque – the courtyard with small rooms off it where travellers stay."

"That's where the old man lived!" said Hani. "The one who told me about the Prisoner being a Messenger of God."

Yunus nodded. "We have been meeting with some of the Prisoner's followers who stay there," he said. "Your mother bakes bread for them sometimes. And I help to get the pilgrims safely into the city at night without the spies finding out."

The Missing Clue

Hani stared open-mouthed at his father, speechless with astonishment!

"That man whose heart was changed by the Prisoner also helps," continued Yunus.

For a moment Hani looked puzzled.

"You know – the one you heard two men talking about in the market," said Yunus. "The shaykh who hid a dagger under his cloak and tried to get into the Prisoner's cell to kill the Prisoner. He has become a devoted believer. He lowers ropes over the wall so pilgrims can climb up and enter the city without being seen by those spies who live above the Land Gate."

He paused and his eyes were full of love as he looked at Hani.

"Why didn't you tell me?" asked Hani, his own eyes filling with tears.

"You and Baz were asking so many questions I thought people would become suspicious, especially that soldier who was keeping such a close eye on you," Yunus gently explained. "And if Salma had heard you talking too much about it, well, she was too young to know she shouldn't mention it to anyone else. All of us could have been in danger. I haven't even told Fuad yet."

I will soon, though, thought Yunus to himself. Fuad was now seventeen years old and a good son, and although he had never shown much interest in religion before, recently he had been asking thoughtful questions about the purpose of life.

Yunus smiled at Hani, whose eyes were now full of excitement, his tears forgotten.

The Missing Clue

"Go and fetch Baz," he said, "and I will tell you both everything I know."

Hani jumped up, and paused in the doorway to look back at his father.

"But His *name*," he said. "The cook at the prison said it is Husayn Alí. It doesn't begin with B."

"But it does," said Yunus with a smile that lit up his face and made his eyes sparkle. "He is known as Bahá'u'lláh!"

Hani gasped. He remembered the clue the elderly dervish had given him, and which, at the time, he had not understood. The dervish had said there was nothing greater than the Glory of God and there was nothing more to be said. In Arabic, Bahá'u'lláh meant the Glory of God!

His Name was the hundredth Name of God!

PART TWO

27

The Ever-Growing Tree

"It's all part of the Covenant of God, something that has been happening since the world began," said Yunus, when Hani and Baz were sitting in front of him on the floor of his workshop. "Like a tree. But one that has been growing for thousands of years."

The Ever-Growing Tree

Hani and Baz wondered what kind of tree Yunus meant.

Yunus smiled. "A spiritual tree," he said, "one that starts as a seed, then grows leaves, buds, flowers, and finally fruit."

The boys were intrigued.

"The tree I am talking about," explained Yunus, "is the religion of God. At the very beginning, thousands of years ago in the time of Adam, when only a tiny bit of the teachings of God were known and it was like a tiny seed, it was still part of the one religion of God. And when another Messenger came and told us more teachings, that was like new leaves appearing. And when the next One came and told us even more, that was like a bud. And so on."

Hani suddenly understood.

"So God didn't tell us everything at the very beginning," he said, "just gradually. Like teachers do in school. A little more each time."

"Exactly," said Yunus. "As people understood more, God told them more by sending another Messenger. They are Divine Teachers."

28

Mirrors of God

"Was Adam the first?" asked Baz.

"He is the first we know of," said Yunus. "That is when we first understood about right and wrong. After Him came Noah who taught us about God."

"Abraham did too," said Hani.

"And Moses," said Baz.

"There were also others who came to different parts of the world," Yunus told them. "Like Krishna, Zoroaster and Buddha. Their teachings spread in far-away places like India, Persia and China."

Baz had never heard of these Messengers of God before and did not think any of their followers lived in 'Akká. It would be interesting to meet them. He knew about Jesus because there were several churches in the town and a friend of his parents had been a Christian before he became a Muslim. He now believed in them both.

"Jesus and Muhammad," he added. "They are from God as well."

"Yes," said Yunus. "They all reflect the light of God, like mirrors reflect the light of the sun. If you turn mirrors towards the sun, you will see the same sun shining in all of them."

"Oh!" said Baz, as everything became clear. "In the same way, you can see God shining in all the Holy Messengers."

"Which means," said Hani thoughtfully, "it would be wrong if you said only one of the Messengers of God was right and not the others, because all of them are."

"None of the Messengers of God ever said that the others were wrong," said Yunus. "And they all promised that the Holy Spirit would return in the future. Unfortunately, every time a new Messenger comes people don't believe Him at first just because He has a different name or appears in a different place."

"Some believe," said Baz quickly. "Like Hani and me. And you, Uncle. And Auntie Pari." He felt worried that his parents did not know about Bahá'u'lláh. When he had told them how he and Hani had found all those clues, they had not said anything.

A Boy in 'Akká - 1868 to 1870

Yunus looked at him kindly. Baz's parents also secretly believed in Bahá'u'lláh and had planned to tell him. Yunus knew they would be happy he was telling their son about Him.

When Yunus was sure the boys understood that there was only one religion that was gradually revealed by different Messengers of God, he said:

"God said He will keep sending His Messengers to the world. It is called the Covenant of God. A promise. Whenever people start forgetting about Him and things go wrong in the world, He sends another Messenger to put things right. It is the only way we know what He wants us to do next. He would never suddenly stop."

29

The Herald

"The story of the latest two Messengers of God began just a few years ago," said Yunus the following day, when all the chores were done and there was an hour to spare before the evening meal. "In 1844, a young man in Persia called the Báb announced that not only was He a new Messenger from God, but He was the Herald of one even greater than Himself."

"What's a herald?" asked Baz, shifting his position slightly to make himself more comfortable. One of his legs had gone to sleep.

"Someone who is the first to tell people something important is about to happen," said Yunus. "In the case of the Báb, He came to make people's hearts pure so they would recognize Bahá'u'lláh when He came."

"What happened to the Báb?" asked Hani. "When He told people that?"

A Boy in 'Akká - 1868 to 1870

Yunus told the boys how the religious leaders and the government had imprisoned the Báb for six years in remote castles in the north of Persia. And his eyes glistened with tears as he described the day the Báb was taken before a firing squad of 750 soldiers and killed.

"He was only 31 years old," he said. "And He was very gentle and kind."

They were all silent, thinking how people always reject the Messengers of God at first. Jesus had been nailed on a cross and left to die. Muhammad had been attacked and his grandchildren killed. Now the Báb had been martyred and Bahá'u'lláh put in prison.

The Herald

After they had eaten, Baz got ready to go home as it was getting late. But Hani had a question. He had been thinking about it all through the meal. It had to do with the name of the Báb. He knew it was an Arabic word for Gate. And a gate always led from one place to another.

"I know my name means...," Hani gave a grin, "happy! And Baz means falcon, and Salma means peace, and Fuad means heart and...," he stopped, thinking that was enough to make his point. "But why was the Báb the Gate?"

Yunus smiled. "One of the reasons was because the Báb was the Gate leading from the great Faiths of the past, which all promised a time of peace, to a time when all these promises would come true through the teachings of Bahá'u'lláh. Now is the time when the whole world will gradually become united for the very first time in history."

Yunus paused, a far-away look in his eyes, then added, "People have been waiting for this time for thousands of years."

"Wow!" said Baz. "And we are alive right now. At this very moment. In the actual time everyone has been praying for!"

30

Bahá'u'lláh in the Siyyáh-Chál

Over a week had passed. Yunus had been too busy to talk with the boys until now and they were desperate to know more.

"What happened to Bahá'u'lláh after the Báb was martyred?" asked Hani, as soon as they were settled.

"Well," said Yunus, "the religious leaders continued to kill thousands of the believers, and two years later they arrested Bahá'u'lláh. He was led barefoot for hours along the dry, dusty road that led to the capital city. His hat was snatched from His head and He had no protection from the fierce heat of the sun. People lined the streets and jeered as He passed, pelting Him with stones. Nobody called out a friendly greeting.

"An old woman stepped forward with a stone in her hand to throw at Him, but she could not keep pace with the procession and He had passed by before she had the chance to do it. She was beside herself with rage and frustration.

"'Give me a chance to fling my stone in His face,' she called out to the guards.

"Although she was so full of anger, Bahá'u'lláh felt a great love for her and did not blame her. He knew she did not understand. He knew she believed what she was doing was right and that it would make her happy. He asked the guards to slow down so she could throw the stone at Him."

Hani and Baz felt lumps in their throats and tried to swallow their tears. Yunus patted their hands and smiled encouragingly.

"That is the special thing about the Messengers of God," he said. "They never stop loving us."

He waited until the boys felt better and then continued.

"When Bahá'u'lláh arrived in Tehran, He was taken to a dungeon called the Siyyáh-Chál, which means the Black Pit. It was the worst prison in the whole of Persia. At first His family did not know where He was, but a

A Boy in 'Akká - 1868 to 1870

servant had seen what had happened and ran to tell them. Before long their house was attacked by gangs who broke down the doors and stole everything inside. His wife and children ran away in fear of their lives."

"How old were His children?" asked Baz, his eyes round with worry. He felt he was with them as they were being chased through the town and his heart beat so wildly it made his chest hurt.

"The oldest was Abbás. He would have been about eight at the time. His sister, Bahíyyih, was six. And little Mihdí no more than three or four," Yunus told him.

"Was Abbás the one I saw in the market?" asked Hani. "The one people call the Master?"

Yunus nodded.

"And was Mihdí the one who died in the prison?" asked Baz.

Yunus nodded again.

And Bahíyyih must have been the young woman I saw two years ago when the prisoners first arrived, thought Hani. The one her brothers had reached out to help when she nearly fainted.

"But something holy happened in that Black Pit," said Yunus, "One of His followers told me."

31

A Light in the Darkness

"Imagine," said Yunus, placing his large hands on his knees and leaning forward to gaze into the eyes of the two boys as they sat unblinking before him. "Imagine having to feel your way in the darkness with no light to show you the way, down three flights of steps deeper and  deeper under the ground. Hearing the groans of the prisoners from the cell below as chains dug into their necks and wrists and ankles every time they moved. The feel of rats scampering over your feet. The smell. The feel of a heavy chain hung around your neck, bowing your head to the dirty ground. The

A Boy in 'Akká - 1868 to 1870

guards laughing as they walk back up the steps and out through the door into the fresh air and sunshine beyond. The loud clunk of the key as they lock the heavy door behind them, plunging the dungeon into the densest darkness. That was the Black Pit where Bahá'u'lláh was imprisoned."

Hani felt goosebumps travelling up his back and into his hair.

"But you said something holy happened there!" he said when he recovered his breath, which he had unconsciously been holding while he listened to his father.

"It did," said Yunus.

He told them how the Black Pit was crowded with more than 150 prisoners, many of them murderers and thieves and the rest innocent followers of the Báb; how, despite the dreadful conditions, Bahá'u'lláh and the believers would chant prayers so loudly and with such joy that the sound travelled up through the ground and could be heard outside; how even the Sháh in his palace heard them chanting.

"Then one night," said Yunus, "when everyone was asleep, Bahá'u'lláh felt the spirit of God filling

A Light in the Darkness

His soul. He said it was like a mighty waterfall pouring over His head from a great height, filling every atom of His being. And then He heard a heavenly voice and saw a vision of an angel shining in the air before Him."

Baz clutched Hani's arm and shut his eyes so he could concentrate and see the angel more clearly in his head.

"Pointing her finger towards Bahá'u'lláh, she said: 'By God! This is the Best-Beloved of the worlds, and yet ye comprehend not. This is the Beauty of God amongst you, and the power of His sovereignty within you, could ye but understand.'"

The three of them sat unmoving in the small workshop. Hani felt they were surrounded by a halo of light and wished they could stay in it for ever.

32

Banished to Baghdad

"Bahá'u'lláh was kept for four months in the Black Pit," Yunus told the boys the following day. "He became very ill because of the dirt and disease. Also, the great weight of the chain round His neck meant that He could not move or even lift His head. He had not slept properly all the time He was there.

"Day by day one or more of the believers had been taken out and shot and now there were only a few left. Everyone thought Bahá'u'lláh would be next. But God had another plan for Him. The government authorities ordered Him to leave Persia and never to return again. On a cold January day in 1853 He was banished from His country forever."

"Where did He go?" asked Hani.

"He set off through the mountains to Baghdad," said Yunus. "It took three months to get there."

"Did Bahá'u'lláh's wife and children go with Him?" asked Baz.

"Well," said Yunus. "His wife was with Him and a few other people, but only two of His children. They tied some belongings to the backs of mules and set off on horseback for the long, uncomfortable journey. It was snowing and bitterly cold. The children's mother had been worried that her youngest child would die on the way, so he was left behind with his great-grandma. He didn't see his parents and brother and sister again until he was eleven."

It was all very sad, thought Hani, imagining how Mihdí must have felt when he had to be left behind. And he shivered as he thought of the icy wind blowing through the mountains.

"It was so cold," said Yunus, "their faces froze and they couldn't move their lips to speak."

33

Everything Made New

"I haven't heard everything that happened when Bahá'u'lláh and His Family arrived in Baghdad," said Yunus. "But I know that near the beginning He spent two years alone praying in the mountains. And that His love attracted hundreds of followers. So many, in fact, that after several years the authorities in Persia got worried and said He should be sent even further away from their border. So they wrote to the Sultan of Turkey asking him to make sure that Bahá'u'lláh moved further north. The people who lived in Baghdad were very upset when He left and many cried."

"Did people know that Bahá'u'lláh was a Messenger of God?" Baz wanted to know. "Did He tell them what God had told Him in the Black Pit?"

"Some of them guessed," said Yunus. "Then, just before He left Baghdad, He stayed in a large garden by the river Tigris, and it was here that He openly said He was the Promised One of all religions."

Everthing Made New

Hani and Baz imagined being in the garden with the other believers. Seeing Bahá'u'lláh as He walked among the roses. Hearing His voice. Seeing Him smile.

Yunus got up and went to a corner of the room and took out a loose brick in the wall. Behind it was a hole with some papers inside. He reverently took out one of the sheets.

"I have to hide these in case the soldiers come and search my house and find them," he explained to the watching boys. "Then we could all be thrown out of town and be homeless."

He placed the paper on his workbench and Hani and Baz gazed at the page of Arabic writing.

"This is a copy of something Bahá'u'lláh wrote," said Yunus. "He says that every time a Messenger of God comes, the world is made new. He says the holy breeze of bounty blows upon all created things."

A Boy in 'Akká - 1868 to 1870

"Over everyone?" asked Hani, to make sure. "Not just the people who were in the garden with Bahá'u'lláh?"

"Everyone," said Yunus. "Us too."

"What year was that, Uncle?" asked Baz. "When Bahá'u'lláh was in the garden and the world became new?"

Yunus thought for a moment as he worked it out. "Seven years ago," he said. "1863."

"When we were five!" said Baz and Hani together.

And they wondered if they had felt different that day when everything in the world, including themselves, had been made new.

34

Knowing With Your Heart

"The Sultan of Turkey demanded that Bahá'u'lláh and His Family should be sent to the capital, Constantinople," said Yunus, several days later when he had time to talk to the boys again.

Baz was impressed. It was his dream to visit Constantinople one day. He had heard it was full of beautiful palaces and grand houses and bazaars selling gold, and that it had a sea called the Bosphorus passing through the middle bringing ships and people from all parts of the world.

"I don't think it is quite as grand as people say!" said Yunus with a smile, noticing the look of wonder on Baz's face. "While some people are very rich, most are too poor to buy enough to eat. And the Sultan lives in fear that one day he will be killed because of the unrest in his country. He thinks the people want to get rid of him and rule themselves."

Baz looked disappointed. "But it would have been nice to have been there with Bahá'u'lláh," he said, sure that would have made all the difference.

"That would have been wonderful," agreed Yunus, and he was silent for a moment as they all thought about it. "But I don't think the Sultan liked the idea of Bahá'u'lláh being in the capital city, so he only allowed Him to stay four months."

"Where was He sent then?" asked Hani, thinking how exhausting it must have been for Bahá'u'lláh and His family to be moved from place to place like this.

"Even further away, to a town right up in the north," said Yunus. "The Sultan was told lies about the Holy Family and this made him frightened. So everyone had to pack up their belongings again and set off on donkeys and carts for Adrianople. It took twelve days to get there and it was so cold that on the way they had to break the ice on the rivers and melt it over a fire in order to have water to drink."

Knowing With Your Heart

"Did Bahá'u'lláh ever get to meet the Sultan?" asked Hani. "Then He could have explained everything, and the Sultan would know he needn't be worried anymore."

"He tried to," said Yunus. "He asked to see the Sultan for just ten minutes to explain His Cause to him, but there was no reply."

Hani sighed and wondered again why the Messengers of God had to suffer. Why people could not at least listen before deciding something was not true. Why they were not even interested in knowing if it was true or not in the first place. That was the most bewildering bit. Then he remembered about his school and how the mullás had been cross with him just for asking questions. And, he thought to himself, they had been very good questions! How could you find the truth if you never asked?

But there was more to it, he decided. It was not a matter of just knowing with your head but with your heart. It was a spiritual knowing. Like he had known as soon as he had seen the prisoners arriving in 'Akká. And the strange thing was, it had just happened without him seeming to do anything about it. He had wanted to follow Bahá'u'lláh up the road and into the prison, and he still had the same feeling.

35

The Wonderful Pilgrim

"Bahá'u'lláh stayed five years in Adrianople," said Yunus. "That's when He began to write to the kings and rulers of the world. He told them about new teachings from God that will help people understand that religion is really one and that God loves everyone and we should all live in peace with one another. During that time He wrote to the Sháh of Persia, the Sultan of Turkey, the Emperor of France and many more."

Yunus told them that not all of the letters had been sent as soon as they were written. There was no reliable postal service at the time and Bahá'u'lláh had to wait until He could find a way for them to be delivered safely.

So some of those letters must have been in the boxes the prisoner's had with them when they first arrived in 'Akká, thought Hani. He had seen them being carried off the boat.

The Wonderful Pilgrim

"Many people offered to take the letter to the Sháh of Persia," continued Yunus. "But Bahá'u'lláh refused. He was waiting for the right person to do it. Then, last year, 1869, He had a visit from a seventeen-year-old boy called Badí who managed to get into 'Akká disguised as a water-carrier. With the help of the Master he was able to get into the fortress twice to see Bahá'u'lláh."

Hani and Baz glanced at each other. That was one pilgrim they had missed seeing.

"During those visits Badí became a different person," said Yunus. "Something spiritual happened to him. Previously he had not always been good or particularly brave, but Bahá'u'lláh changed him completely. His heart became so full of the love of God that he wasn't afraid of anything."

Hani felt a spark of that love in his own heart and was filled with a warm glow. He looked at Baz and knew from his face that he was feeling the same thing too.

"Bahá'u'lláh chose Badí to take the letter to the Sháh," said Yunus. "And he left at once. He kissed the box containing the important letter and set off on foot for Persia. It took him several months to get there."

Yunus fell silent. News had just come that Badí had managed to give the letter to the Sháh, but he had been chained and imprisoned by the guards, and then been martyred.

"His name means wonderful," he said, softly.

36

A Vision Come True

There was just one more thing Yunus wanted to say.

"Bahá'u'lláh wrote something very interesting about His arrival in 'Akká," he said.

He looked intently at Hani and read:

> "Upon Our arrival, We were welcomed with banners of light, whereupon the Voice of the Spirit cried out saying: 'Soon will all that dwell on earth be enlisted under these banners.'"

Hani gasped. He could hardly believe his ears.

"Oh!" he said, remembering the lights he thought he had seen in the sky two years before. He had begun to doubt they had ever existed as no one else had seen them. Now he knew why. They had not been ordinary lights at all but something spiritual from the next world.

A Boy in 'Akká - 1868 to 1870

He looked at his father and Baz and smiled, full of awe at the wonder of things.

"Can I tell Salma the story of Bahá'u'lláh?" he asked, not wanting his sister to be left out, especially as she had been part of the discovery of the plaque and already knew quite a lot.

Yunus hesitated, still not sure whether she was old enough to understand how careful she would have to be. After all, 'Akká was a prison-city and there were soldiers and spies everywhere.

He was still wondering what to say when there was a creak as the heavy door of the workroom slowly opened and Salma's smiling face appeared. She had come to tell them the evening meal was ready and had overheard Hani's question. She looked hopefully at her father, her eyes shining.

Yunus's heart melted.

"Of course," he said.

37

Under the Stars

It was a warm summer night, and Hani, Salma, Baz and Fuad were on the flat roof of Baz's house. They were lying on their backs and gazing at the stars. Whole families used to sleep on the rooftops in summer as it was cooler than being inside, and hundreds of candles were flickering on tops of houses all over the city.

The parents of the children were having a meeting in a room below and would join them later. The sound of Pari chanting a prayer floated up through an open window.

"Perhaps you'll have another vision!" said Baz to Hani when it finished.

"You can't make them happen!" laughed Hani. "They just come, like dreams. Anyway," he said, "that vision led us to Bahá'u'lláh, so I don't need to have another one!"

A Boy in 'Akká - 1868 to 1870

"What do we do now?" asked Salma. "Now that we know about Bahá'u'lláh?"

"Well," said Fuad, who had been thinking seriously ever since his father had spent the last two days explaining things to him. "We have to try to do what Bahá'u'lláh says."

"Like loving people," said Hani, his eyes lit by the stars that seemed to go on for ever.

"Being kind," said Baz.

"Being fair," said Salma.

"Being friendly with followers of all religions," said Fuad.

"Bahá'u'lláh has come to unite everybody in the world," said Hani.

"Like one big family," said Salma, smiling to herself in the dark, and thinking how much she loved Bahá'u'lláh who had brought such beautiful teachings.

"No more wars," said Baz.

"Just peace," said Hani.

And he heard the sound of millions of stars singing.

- The End -

Under the Stars

Selected Words of Bahá'u'lláh

"In this Day a great festival is taking place
in the Realm above;
for whatsoever was promised in the sacred Scriptures
hath been fulfilled.
This is the Day of great rejoicing.
It behoveth everyone to hasten towards the
court of His nearness
with exceeding joy, gladness, exultation and delight...."

"Incline your ears
to the sweet melody of this Prisoner.
Arise, and lift up your voices,
that haply they that are fast asleep
may be awakened...."

"This is the Call of the All-Glorious
which is proclaimed ... in the Prison of 'Akká....

O people! Consort with the followers of all religions
in a spirit of friendliness and fellowship."

Meeting Bahá'u'lláh

"Sixteen lunar months, less twenty and two days,
had elapsed since the day of the martyrdom
of the Báb,
when ... my eyes, for the first time,
fell upon Bahá'u'lláh.
What shall I recount regarding the countenance
which I beheld! The beauty of that face,
those exquisite features which no pen or brush
dare describe, His penetrating glance,
His kindly face,
the majesty of His bearing,
the sweetness of His smile,
the luxuriance of His jet-black flowing locks,
left an indelible impression upon my soul....
From that moment all my sorrows vanished.
My soul was flooded with joy."

(Words of a believer named Shaykh Hasan-i-Zunúzí, who met Bahá'u'lláh in Karbila in 1851)

A Short History of Bahá'u'lláh

Bahá'u'lláh is the Founder of the Bahá'í Faith. He was born in 1817 in Tihrán, the capital of Persia (Irán). From His early childhood He showed signs of greatness. He did not need to attend school, for God had given Him the knowledge of all things. He came from a noble family, and when he was a young man he was offered a high position in the court of the King, but He refused it. He wished to spend His time in helping the sad, the sick and the poor, and supporting the cause of justice.

His suffering began the moment He arose to proclaim the Cause of God. His life was one of exile, imprisonment and persecution. He was put in chains in a dark and dismal dungeon in Tihrán. He was exiled four times from land to land, finally being sent to the Prison City of 'Akká in the Ottoman Empire. This was the most terrible prison at that time and no one was expected to live long after being sent there.

Two powerful kings – the Sháh of Persia and the Sultan of the Ottoman Empire – opposed Bahá'u'lláh and His teachings. They wanted to destroy the new religion. But the more the authorities banished Him, the greater the number of people who were attracted to His teachings and recognized His power and majesty. In spite of constant persecution, Bahá'u'lláh continued to reveal the Word of God for more than forty years and brought a great love and spiritual energy into the world.

He passed away, still a prisoner, in 1892, and is buried near the city of 'Akká.

Some Teachings of Bahá'u'lláh

All religions promised a time when a Great One from God would come to bring peace and harmony to the world. Bahá'ís believe that Bahá'u'lláh is that Promised One and that through Him the Holy Spirit of God has returned to gather together all mankind. He explains that all the world religions have come from God at different stages in the history of man and now is the time for us to travel on together, for the world is one country and mankind its citizens. There are now millions of people from every country in the world who have become Bahá'ís.

Among other teachings of Bahá'u'lláh are the harmony of religion and science; the equality of men and women; the elimination of extremes of wealth and poverty; the need for every girl and boy to be educated; belief in life after death; that everyone should search for truth; and a new system to bring peace and justice to the world.

"Bahá'u'lláh has drawn the circle of unity, He has made a design for the uniting of all the peoples, and for the gathering of them all under the shelter of the tent of universal unity."

('Abdu'l-Bahá)

Bibliography

'Abdu'l-Bahá. *'Abdu'l-Bahá in London*. Bahá'í Publishing Trust: London, 1982.

—*Selections from the Writings of 'Abdu'l-Bahá*. Bahá'í World Centre: Haifa, 1978.

Bahá'u'lláh. *Epistle to the Son of the Wolf*. Bahá'í Publishing Trust: Wilmette, 1941.

—*Gleanings from the Writings of Bahá'u'lláh*. Bahá'í Publishing Trust: London, 1978.

—*The Hidden Words*. Bahá'í Publishing Trust: London, 1975.

—*Kitáb-i-Aqdas: The Most Holy Book*. Bahá'í World Centre: Haifa, 1992.

—*Kitáb-i-Íqán: The Book of Certitude*. Bahá'í Publishing Trust: London, 1946.

—*The Summons to the Lord of Hosts:* Bahá'í World Centre: Haifa, 2002.

—*Tablets of Bahá'u'lláh: Revealed after the Kitáb-í-Aqdas*. Bahá'í World Centre: Haifa, 1978.

Balyuzi, H. M. *Bahá'u'lláh: The King of Glory*. George Ronald: Oxford, 1980.

Esslemont, J. E. *Bahá'u'lláh and the New Era*. Bahá'í Publishing

Bibliography

Trust: London, 1974.

Holy Bible, The. Authorised King James Version. London.

Nabíl-i-Azam. *The Dawn-Breakers: Nabil's Narrative of the Early Days of the Bahá'í Revelation.* Bahá'í Publishing Trust: Wilmette, 1962; also Bahá'í Publishing Trust: London, 1953.

Qur'án [Koran]. Trans. J. M. Rodwell. London: Dent (Everyman's Library), 1963.

Shoghi Effendi. *God Passes By.* Wilmette: Bahá'í Publishing Trust, 1957.

—*High Endeavours: Messages to Alaska* (Letters from and on behalf of Shoghi Effendi). Published by the National Spiritual Assembly of the Bahá'ís of Alaska, 1976.

—*Letters from the Guardian to Australia and New Zealand 1923-1957.* Published by the Bahá'ís of Australia Incorporated, 1970.

References and Notes

The 99 Names of God (chs. 8, 9, 23)
A famous Tradition says: "To God belongs 99 names, 100 minus 1. Anyone who memorizes them will enter Paradise." The hundredth Name was said to be hidden and was especially holy and would not be revealed until the Day of Judgement, the Day of Resurrection, the Great Announcement. Bahá'u'lláh says that Day has now come.

Prophecies about 'Akká (chs. 5, 26, 36)
"And I will give her ... the valley of Achor for a door of hope: and she shall sing there, as in the days of her youth, and as in the day when she came up out of the land of Egypt." (Bible, Hosea 2.15)

"This valley of Achor is the city of 'Akká ...." (*Selections from the Writings of 'Abdu'l-Bahá*, no. 139, p. 163).

"The Apostle of God ... is reported to have said: 'Blessed the man that hath visited 'Akká, and blessed he that hath visited the visitor of 'Akká.'" (Bahá'u'lláh, *Epistle to the Son of the Wolf*, p. 179)

"'I bring you tidings of a city betwixt two mountains in Syria, in the middle of a meadow, which is called 'Akká. Verily, he that entereth therein, longing for it and eager to visit it, God will forgive his sins, both of the past and of the future.... In it is a spring called the Spring of the Cow. Whoso drinketh a draught therefrom, God will fill his heart with light, and will protect him from the most great terror on the Day of Resurrection.'" (Baha'u'llah, quoting the words of Ibn-i-Mas'úd, one of the early Arab Muslims at the time of Muhammad, in *Epistle to the Son of the Wolf*, p. 178)

"Upon Our arrival We were welcomed with banners of light, whereupon the Voice of the Spirit cried out saying: 'Soon will all that dwell on

References and Notes

earth be enlisted under these banners.'" (Bahá'u'lláh, quoted by Shoghi Effendi in *God Passes By*, ch. Xl, p.184.)

Station of Bahá'ú'lláh (chs. 14, 19, 27, 28, 31)
"Pointing her finger towards Bahá'u'lláh, she said: 'By God! This is the Best-Beloved of the worlds, and yet ye comprehend not. This is the Beauty of God amongst you, and the power of His sovereignty within you, could ye but understand.'" (Bahá'u'lláh, *The Summons of the Lord of Hosts*, Suriy-i-Haykal, p. 6, v. 7)

"To Israel He was neither more nor less than the incarnation of the 'Everlasting Father', the 'Lord of Hosts' come down 'with ten thousands of saints'; to Christendom Christ returned 'in the glory of the Father', to Shí'áh Islam the return of the Imam Husayn; to Sunni Islam the descent of the 'Spirit of God' (Jesus Christ); to the Zoroastrians the promised Sháh-Bahrám; to the Hindus the reincarnation of Krishna; to the Buddhists the fifth Buddha." (Shoghi Effendi, *God Passes By*, ch. Vl, p. 94)

Oneness of God and Religion: Progressive Revelation (chs. 10, 27, 28)
"Every one of them [the Messengers of God] is a mirror of God, reflecting naught else but His Self, His Beauty, His Might and Glory...." (*Gleanings from Writings of Bahá'u'lláh*, no. XXX)

"Today, the bud is unfolding into a flower! Bahá'u'lláh has expanded and fulfilled the teachings, and has applied them in detail to the whole world." (*'Abdu'l-Bahá in London*, pp. 92-93)

"Him [Bahá'u'lláh] Whose Cause is the flower and fruit of all previous Revelations." (Shoghi Effendi, *God Passes By*, ch. Vll, p. 107)

"The bud, the flower, the fruit are only symbols to convey to us the sense of the progress being made by man in receiving ever fuller Revelations from God. In spite of the vast spiritual significance of what Bahá'u'lláh has brought to the world we humans have infinite progress to make in the future. Future Prophets will bring us new laws suitable to our state of development and continue to educate us on this planet, but they will be under the shadow of Bahá'u'lláh for five thousand centuries." (Shoghi Effendi, *High Endeavours - Messages to Alaska*, p. 71)

A Boy in 'Akká - 1868 to 1870

"The religion of God is the One Religion, and all the Prophets have taught it, but it is a living and a growing thing.... The flower does not destroy the bud, nor does the fruit destroy the flower. It destroys not, but fulfils." (J. E. Esslemont, *Bahá'u'lláh and the New Era*, ch. 8, p.118)

Everything Made New (chs. 33, 36)
"Thus it is that through the rise of these Luminaries of God [the Messengers of God] the world is made new." (Bahá'u'lláh, *The Kitáb-i-Iqán*, p. 34)

"Verily, all created things were immersed in the sea of purification when, on that first day of Riḍván, We shed upon the whole of creation the splendours of Our most excellent Names and Our most exalted Attributes." (Bahá'u'lláh, *The Kitáb-i-Aqdas*, p. 47, v.75)

"...in one of His specific Tablets, He has referred to it as the Day whereon 'the breezes of forgiveness were wafted over the entire creation'." (Shoghi Effendi, *God Passes By*, ch. IX, p. 154)

The Báb (ch. 29)
"Though young and tender of age, and though the Cause He revealed was contrary to the desire of all the peoples of earth, yet He arose and steadfastly proclaimed it." "The more severe the persecution ..., the more His fervour increased, and the brighter burned the flame of His love ...." (Bahá'u'lláh, *The Kitáb'-i-Iqán*, pp. 230 and 233-4)

The Master (chs. 21, 22)
The oldest son of Bahá'u'lláh. When He was born He was called Abbás, but when He was older Bahá'u'lláh called Him the Master. Later, after the passing of His Father, the Master asked to be called 'Abdu'l-Bahá (which means the Servant of Bahá'u'lláh). Bahá'u'lláh said that the Master was the perfect example of how a Bahá'í should be and that we should all turn to Him for guidance.

Some Words of Bahá'u'lláh (quoted after chapter 37)
"In this Day a great festival ... exultation and delight...." (*Tablets of Bahá'u'lláh*, Kalimat-i-Firdawsiyyih, pp. 78-79)

References and Notes

"Incline your ears ... may be awakened...." (*Gleanings from the Writings of Bahá'u'lláh*, no. CVI, p. 212)

"This is the Call of the All-Glorious ... friendliness and fellowship." (*Tablets of Bahá'u'lláh*, Bishárát, pp. 21-22)

Meeting Bahá'u'lláh (quotation near the end)
"Sixteen lunar months ... flooded with joy." (Nabíl, *The Dawn-Breakers*, Am. ed. p.32; Brit. ed. pp. 24-25)